Ultimate Guide to Learning
Skateboarding Later in Life

LATER SKATER

Breaking Down Barriers of Entry for Later Skaters

MARKO KOSTA

Founder of SK8 GYM

LATER SKATER

Copyrights © 2024 by Marko Kosta

All Rights Reserved

The scanning, uploading, and distribution of this book without permission is a theft of the authors intellectual property. If you would like permission to use materials from the book (Other than for review purposes), please contact info@sk8gym.com. Thank you for your support of the authors rights.

First edition: January 2024

Cover design by Brian DiNonno

I would like to dedicate this book to the following people:

My Parents: you both always encouraged and supported me in following my passions and along the way, gently reminded me that skateboarding would get me nowhere in life.

My Wife: Your love and support of SK8 GYM has given me the opportunity to set aside time to write this guide. I love you!

Acknowledgements

My Students: You all changed my life completely. I honestly could not be more grateful for all the opportunities that you have given me to refine my skateboarding curriculum.

Table of Contents

INTRODUCTION 1
PART ONE: Muscle Memory and Body Conditioning 3
    LOW IS PRO 5
    OH NO, GET LOW 7
    BURNING IS LEARNING 9
PART TWO: Technique Building 13
    ZEN IS 10 15
    HOCUS FOCUS 18
    EYES ON THE PRIZE 20
PART THREE: Course of Learning 23
    PAR WITH A CAR 25
    STICK THE TRICK 27
PART FOUR: Refinement and Perseverance 31
    TWO TO MAKE IT TRUE 33
    NO PAIN, NO GAIN 35
ABOUT THE AUTHOR 37

INTRODUCTION

Trying skateboarding for the first time in your adulthood can be a scary proposition, albeit one that sounds really fun, assuming no significant injuries occur in the process. The fear of falling or getting hurt as an adult is REAL and can stem from a variety of different concerns. From "I can't remember the last time I fell" to "I have a job and need to pay bills, I can't afford to get injured and loss time from work" or "I have family to feed and care for" or "I don't have medical insurance" or "I never tried it in my youth" or "I'm not in the proper physical shape" or "I simply don't want to fall and get hurt." These fears hold formidable barriers to some of the most fun anybody can possibly have in this world and let's not forget the amazing workout that comes along with skating. This guide aims to lower the barriers of entry for first-time adults trying skateboarding. In order to break-through the fears and achieve your goal to try and eventually enjoy the many different types of positive attributes skateboarding provides, there are two distinct roads one can traverse in their journey. To enlist the help a skateboard coach or not. Ideally, the adult will take the wise route and hire a skate coach right from the start to keep themselves as safe as possible while having fun, avoid building bad habits, learning, and even to do so before investing in a skateboard and protective gear. Understanding which gear to buy and not buy is also crucial to safe progression.

There are four activates that help tremendously with speeding up the skateboarding learning process. Skateboard is a mix of these four disciplines: martial arts, gymnastics, parkour, and dancing, particularly dancing forms that rely heavily on the toes, like ballet.

A late pro skater named Zane Timpson, who also happen to instruct skateboarding for SK8 GYM, coined skateboarding as "aggressive ballet." I have had adult students who were new to skateboarding, but not new to martial arts, gymnastics or some combination of those four activities and in my experience, their skateboarding progression is on average faster than others, even if their learning style is on the lower end of the effectiveness scale.

There are typically three steps to learning new tricks. Step 1. On-carpet, Step 2. Off-carpet and Step 3. Dynamic off-carpet. This process only applies to some tricks. Many tricks cannot be performed stationary and thus are not included in steps 1 and 2. Good news for you is that many of the basic tricks can be executed in all three parts. Learning tricks using this three-step process is key to safe progression early on in your traning.

PART ONE: Muscle Memory and Body Conditioning

LOW IS PRO

In skateboarding there is arguably nothing more important than staying low. Low is pro is a fundamental technique and premeditated movement where you initiate compression at your knees to absorb shock at the exact moment of landing a move or "trick," as it's commonly called. As you intend to stay on your board you start to compress at your knees at just the right time, much like a gymnast would as they stick their landing in order to stay on their feet. Bending at the knees and relying heavily on your quad muscles is crucial for staying on your board and your safety. Think martial arts stance. Getting low can cancel out up to 90-95% of any improper skating techniques and help you recover enough to stay on your board. It can be anything from jumping on your board with both feet at the same time and landing squarely over the screws (also known as bolts) with both feet at the same time or at the moment your front wheels hit the ground from basic tricks like kick-turns, or when placing your back foot on board after taking a push. It plays a role in everything you do on a skateboard with two feet on. Compress to avoid a mess. Compressing at the knees required your back to be mostly straight with your head over the board, chest out, chin up, eyes down or out and arms up, out to the sides or down. Think ballet. Your quads should be burning. Don't forget lots of toe pressure. Try not to bend at your hips. Compressing at the knees can be tricky. It may feel like your compressing quite a bit, but in actuality, you're very likely not compressing enough. There's often a significant gap between perception and reality with this technique. The terms I use to associate the varying degrees of compression is "froggy," either "half froggy" for halfway low or "¾ froggy" for most of the way low or "full froggy" for getting as low as you possibly can, being in a squatting "cannonball like" position. In this position you can use your hands on the ground to help with recovery. During lessons you will be shown when each of these froggy positions are best utilized. Being able to skate tucked into the smallest possible position you can get yourself in, while holding your board with your back hand in front of you (between your feet) and pointing the other arm and your head in the direction you want to go. Try it at home, on a piece of carpet, how small can you make yourself on a board? Being shorter is better than being taller. Being lighter on your feet is better than the alternative. The optimal adult height to learn skateboarding is in the range of 5' 2" – 5' 8". The optimal weight for learning skateboarding is in the range of 110 -160 lbs. Any taller or shorter, lighter or heavier, it starts to work against you as a new skater, aka L8R SK8R.

OH NO, GET LOW

When you feel like you're about to fall off your skateboard, it's time to initiate "Oh No, Get Low" in a crash preparation sequence. Think parkour. This fundamental and spontaneous technique is very similar to Low is Pro by how you physically start compression at the knees. However, it does differ from Low is Pro in some ways. Mentally, it is the complete opposite of Low is Pro in that you know you are likely to fall at the moment and you're no longer intentionally trying to stay on your board. Oh No, Get Low will minimize the impact of the fall, thereby minimizing injury and pain. Practicing Low is Pro also reinforces Oh No, Get Low and in a lesser degree, vice-versa. You can say the two techniques are first cousins. On No, Get Low technique is not easy to refine, it takes a good amount of drills to get your mind used to executing this movement when in peril. The human body's natural instinct during moments of fear is to straighten out. Just think of the cartoon characters who do this when afraid. The natural instinct is the complete opposite of what needs to be done, making it an uphill battle for most to learn. Be patient and you'll get the hang of it. Your skate lessons will include this drill to safely refine your reflexes as timely execution of this technique is crucial in order to effectively accomplish its goal as well as which fall break techniques to use in different scenarios. Think parkour. Falling and sliding out on your knee pads is crucial for your safety. Our brain is wired to never ever fall on our knees. Another example of a technique that will take time to drill in. Try falling straight to your knees with good knee pads on. Remember that wearing a helmet and full pads is a critical safety aspect of this technique. Without it, the benefit of On No, Get Low is outweighed by its detriment. As you improve your skating ability and depending on your skating terrain, you may start moving away from Oh No, Get Low. If you start improving transition skating (i.e. ramps and bowls), Oh No, Get Low will continue to be virtuous. However, for street skating, you will also start learning how to bail landing on your feet. Using the front part of your feet (toes and ball of your feet as the first point of contact with the ground) to bail off your board and jogging or running it off in small steps is useful when you're not attempting big street moves, but rather smaller ones that you will likely stick with in your later skater skateboarding journey. Think ballet. In general terms, your lessons will include some technique switching from early on that will eventually evolve with your progression. When skating ramps, check your shoulder angles. Your shoulders angle should match the ramp angle. So much of your balance on ramps is predicated on matching shoulder and ramp angles. Many later skaters are not interested in riding ramps, but many of my students get good enough to start trying it.

BURNING IS LEARNING

In order to condition your body enough to optimize Low is Pro and Oh No, Get Low as well as other techniques mentioned in later chapters, SK8 GYM training is highly useful. This is the basis for the name of our company. Burning is Learning lives at the core of what safe skateboarding requires. When you feel the burn, you can rest assured that you're learning and staying safer. Now, you may be in great physical condition with disciplined workout regimens, however the best SK8 conditioning techniques involve a skateboard. The reason is, as you condition your body with a board, both your mind and body start developing a physiological connection to your board. This connection is crucial to fusing the board to your mind and body, ultimately becoming one with the board which is possible even at the beginner level. Burning is Learning manifests itself in a variety of ways.

Stretching: Stretching is a critical part of skateboarding safety. I recommend stretching every day and especially before each skateboarding session. I recommend dynamic stretching exercises including arm circles, leg swings, high kicks, high knee, and hip stretch with twist.

Warming up helps minimize injury. 90%+ of all beginner injuries occur in the first 15 minutes of the skating session. Get the heart rate up, blood flowing faster and muscles fired up. Take 10-15 minutes and it doesn't necessarily require the use of a board, but it helps to include a board.

Body conditioning will help improve the rate of your skateboarding progression. It's hard to get good at skateboarding before you build your skateboarding body. There are three important types of conditioning: endurance, core, and quad strength. If you exercise often, whether it's playing sports, dancing, running/ jogging, or any other aerobic exercise, that will help build endurance. Skateboarding requires endurance, otherwise you will struggle to keep up with it. Core strength is also important, specifically for your overall balance. I recommend getting a balance board as it's a fun way to build your core and balance simultaneously on a board. *Indo Board* makes good balance boards. Using a balance board on carpet helps with overall safety, providing traction for the roller. Having someone spot your wrist or using a handle, something with which to brace yourself is also helpful as you get the hang of it. For your quads, the best technique to apply is wall squats. Developing a significant amounts of upper body muscle doesn't help for a couple of reasons. Muscle is heavy, heavier than fat and you don't use your upper body for power in skateboarding. In addition, bending the upper body with extra upper body muscle is tougher to accomplish.

Hydration is so important for safety and overall success. Stay hydrated and always have plenty of water with you when skating. Sip water often, and avoid guzzling. Listen to your body.

PART TWO: Technique Building

ZEN IS 10

Skateboarding requires hyper-focus. If you ever tried meditating, you know what I mean. Skateboarding is so hard that you can't afford to think about anything other than what you are trying to perform on your board, hence Zen is 10. In meditation, that's called singular focus, when you only think of one thing, in our case, that thing is landing the trick or maneuver without getting injured. When you meditate, typically, you don't really worry about getting hurt, so it can be harder to train your mind in the absence of adversity. The fact that your mind is fighting fear is a wonderful motivator to refine your focus, but this fear can also decrease your confidence. Working on increasing overall confidence will minimize the negative affects of fear factor on focus.

A good test of self-preservation is to attempt a fairly simple trick you are learning and do it near a wall, rail or anything that you can reach to brace against or grab. I've seen so many students struggle to not use reach and grab/ brace even though they trust this support is unnecessary. Learning to refrain from reach and grab/ brace can be harder than you think (it's like a knee-jerk reaction) and crucial to lowering your self-preservation levels to promote improved progression.

Reaching works against you as it will very likely disrupt your proper weight distribution.

What's scarier is easier and what's not scary is difficult. There are so many tricks that require higher speed in order to get through the trick so fast that it feels easier and doesn't become some elaborate balancing act. Fear is a formidable foe in skateboarding. Battling fear is the toughest part of skating. When skating, pretend like you're surrounded by bad guys trying to hurt you, it will help keep you safe. Fear leads to hesitation, hesitation leads to leaning back, and that leads to falling and falling can result in getting hurt. Bravery leads to confidence, confidence leads to success and success is less likely to lead to getting hurt. Believe it or not, having the guts to commit is less likely to lead to a bad fall than hesitating somewhere all the attempt. You can be scared and brave at the same time. This is similar to soldiers going to war. Skateboarding is akin to battling. Skateboarding skill can only improve with a direct correlation to increased confidence. It's so challenging to build confidence on a board from the ground up. Those smallest pieces of skateboarding are where it all starts. Our instructional program "Learn to Skate," for those who don't have more than a couple of weeks of experience, start with these ground-breaking steps.

Conversely, if your confidence gets too high, it's very much like being on cloud nine and you can easily misinterpret this for a reason to try something way out of your skill ability or something within your ability, but when you're severely fatigued and need rest. As your coach, I can gradually improve your confidence, keep it high, see when your confidence is too high and will keep you better grounded, feeling good nonetheless.

HOCUS FOCUS

The most difficult part of Hocus Focus in skateboarding is when, where and how much focus is directed. From a focus standpoint, it's important not to get too far ahead of yourself. Keeping the majority or all of your focus on what you're doing in the moment will help keep you safe. If you end up messing up a trick or maneuver that you otherwise have on lock (meaning you consistently perform it well), it's very likely that your focus turned away from it too soon. Whether your focus was diverted away from your skating by some external factor or the more likely culprit, fear or concern of what's coming up next (i.e. the trick) drove you to move your focus to it prematurely, thereby failing the maneuver you are performing at the moment, even those maneuver that you otherwise confidently have on-lock.

There are times when you need to divert your focus from what's happening at the moment with both feet on the board, but just a bit of focus diversion here and there. These fleeting moments of focal diversion from the here and now on your board is required so that you don't run into something or to get a read on your skating environment or your navigation or to size up the upcoming trick. Using your peripheral vision is crucial in many cases as that allows you to keep the majority of your focus on what you're doing at the moment. Where you set your sights is so important for your balance when executing tricks. Optimal sights target are a personal preference, some prefer to look down with an emphasis on observing the board and feet in action. Others do better when their eyes are set down and a little out from the feet/ board, while others prefer to look more straight out than down. Try these options and see for yourself which works best for you. Also, when you turn your head for navigation purposes it's important that your eyes don't always need to be looking in the direction your head is facing. Practice turning your head left, right, up and down and keeping your eyes in a straight-ahead fixed position. It's similar to an eye exam exercise.

Also, stay vigilant and be aware of any debris in your path, clear the space first. You will eventually get jammed by a pebble or something, it's inevitable. Having bigger and softer wheels at first will help you learn the technique without worrying about getting jammed, but soon enough you'll want the smaller harder wheels as they provide a larger margin of error when the wheels can slide on the ground to help complete a turn where soft wheels work against in these moments.

EYES ON THE PRIZE

There are four types of learners, so-called approaches to learning skateboarding.

1. **Thinkers**: This is the toughest learning style. The more you think the more you allow fear to narrate the story and it isn't going to end well, if it even initiates. The higher percentage you are a thinker, the faster skateboarding will exit your life, due to a nasty hobby ending slam, but not if you have a coach. Many students come to me to help them break through the thinking, quiet the mind, and we talk it through, it's much like a therapy session before a trick attempt. Although I don't consider myself a therapist.
2. **Feelers**: This is me, roughly 75% of my learning style. Feelers need to feel it out first, it can turn into lots of bailing…over and over again, sometimes to the point of begging the question, do you even have any intention of landing on your board and stick the trick or just to keep landing on your feet? Skateboarding was hard for me being mostly a feeler. I had to work harder at it than most of my skate mates.

3. **Watcher**: This is me, roughly 25%, watchers have a high probability of success just by watching others do it. The higher the percentage of a watcher you are, the more likely you will want to skate in bigger groups and with those who are better than you. One has the ability to become a pro if they're a high percentage watcher.
4. **Doers**: Most pros come from this group. Doers don't think, they don't need to feel it out, or even watch someone else do it, they simply try what they want to try and commit to it often. This leads to much falling. The more you fall the faster you learn. This group is fearless and confident, so the falls tend to be controlled to a large degree, however that comes with the occasional bone injuries. One thing to watch out for in this group is confidence getting too high which can lead to gassing oneself to the point of trying something way out of their league.

You'll want to assess yourself over time and try to identify which learning category or categories you fit into. As your coach, I can help you analyze. This will give you perspective as to where on the learning scale you reside.

PART THREE: Course of Learning

PAR WITH A CAR

There are a few similarities to riding a skateboarding one can draw from driving a car. While skateboarding might be new to you, chances are, driving a car is not. Understanding the physics of how a car functions and the skill of how someone operates it will help you understand and remember a few key takeaways. First, let's look at **focus**. How often and how much do you divert your focus from the road in front of you. Not much, but when you do it's for only one second and eyes back on the road in front of you. You need to check your mirrors to assess your environment, glancing at your dashboard for speed checks, and looking over your shoulder before changing lanes. Next, let's explore **navigation**. Ever notice the wheel configuration on a skateboard is the same as a car? Why does that even matter, you ask? When you parallel park a car, you do it backwards (or fakie as backwards is referred to in skateboarding) because fakie is a whole lot easier than parallel parking forward. The same for turning on a skateboard. Fakie turns are generally easier, therefore many skateboard turning tricks are first learned moving fakie before learning it moving forward. This may seem counterintuitive since we mostly skate forward and feel more comfortable skating forward. This is a good reason why getting comfortable going fakie early on in your training is crucial, much like how its required to perform parallel parking during your driving test. Now, let's examine **speed**. The speed at which you drive is something that is constantly top of mind when driving. Are you driving the speed limit? Are you driving so slowly that the driver behind you is getting impatient? Is your speed optimal for the car's MPG? Speed should be top of mind for skateboarding as much as it is for driving. Managing speed control is one of the most underrated skateboarding skillsets. Knowing exactly how much speed you need for a particular move or trick will dramatically improve your odds of success. Everything on a skateboard is learned small, slow and low, tricks which require higher speed are learned later. Trying a dynamic trick moving slowly up a slight incline is easier to learn because your losing speed and it doesn't feel as scary. Try to avoid learning new tricks headed into a downhill, as you gain speed, fear can start setting in. Lastly, let's check out **runway**. The amount of runway you have to stop safely in a car is important. It's tied closely to speed. In skateboarding, the amount of runway you take in combination with your optimal speed is crucial for the amount of time it takes to fix your feet after pushing for optimal speed and for timely focus switch to the upcoming trick execution. How fast you can push is also a factor in your trick selections.

STICK THE TRICK

Bookends: It's important to create mental bookends so that you can identify where the sweet spot is located for a particular trick landing. This is done by failing at least twice per trick, once by going too much, too far, too fast or compressing too soon and the other by not going enough, for example, leaning too far back, going too slow or compressing too late.

Body rotation: When you are turning heel-side on your board it is harder than turning toe-side. Heel-side turning is essentially turning toward your back. It's not necessarily called "backside" as this turning direction can also be "frontside," all depending on how you approach or mount an obstacle. Heel-side turns require turning you head all the way in the direction you're turning. The body wants to go in the direction the head is pointed to. If your head is turned all the way toward your heels, the turning will feel much easier. Also, the upper body takes longer to turn than your lower body. Allowing the upper body to get a head start in turning will guarantee it completes the turn at the same time as the lower body. Winding up the upper body helps.

Feet placement on a board is crucial. Set yourself up for success by having your feet placed in the optimal positions for the maneuver you're attempting. Be picky about your feet placement, if feet positioning is off by just a half inch, it could be the difference between success and failure.

Weight distribution is crucial for skateboarding. Your upper body weight is either working to your benefit or it's to your detriment. There is no middle ground here. Learning how to make sure your body weight is on your team will keep you safer and more successful on a board. You'll also be working smarter not harder. Many people apply the theory that hard work pays off, however, in skateboarding the harder you work, the more it involves bad technique that reduces your overall safety on a board. Putting in the work needs to be in a smarter way.

Muscle fatigue: strength and energy build when skateboarding. Strength training also increases endurance, allowing you to skate for longer intervals and minimize injury from muscle fatigue. Only you know when you need to stop for a break. While you should push yourself out of your comfort zone a bit each time to build strength, energy and endurance, too much fatigue will likely result in sustaining injury. Try not to learn this the hard way, be conservative at first and take frequent breaks until you get a better sense of how your body reacts to muscle fatigue.

Margin of error: giving yourself a larger margin of error as you learn will keep you safer. This applies to everything on a skateboard, from pushing to executing tricks. Again, work smarter.

PART FOUR: Refinement and Perseverance

TWO TO MAKE IT TRUE

In order to know with a high degree of accuracy that you have learned a trick, it's important to do it at least twice. Your first successful attempt could have been a fluke or beginner's luck. I can't tell you how many times I unintentionally landed a trick while intending to land a different, but similar trick. Or in the process of losing my balance during a trick, I somehow miraculously regain it and ride away from the trick by dumb luck. There are so many ways to luckily land a skateboarding trick, sometimes you might not even realize it was landed by accident.

Accomplishing your trick at least twice provides strong evidence that the achievement was mostly if not all related to skill and had little to no relation to luck. You can continue to refine your trick mastery beyond this stage by revisiting it every so often. It's a tall order to be a perfectionist on a skateboard. Many skaters like to have their tricks on lock, but it's not always attainable. Skateboarding is a fine art, like playing a musical instrument. It takes so much practice to refine this craft, progress and achieve your goals. I've witnessed friends trying a trick the entire day and after so many gnarly slams over and over again, the relentless pursuit of the elusive trick they have set their sights on takes a toll on their body and spirit. When they finally land it and roll away, it's the most epic feeling, one that I can only compare to experiencing the best feeling in the world. I've had the fortunate of experiencing a wide variety of amazing feelings in my life, but they all pale in comparison to sticking tricks I've been attempting for a while. There are some exceptions to Two to Make it True. When you put your body through the grinder with countless tries, most of which can result in wounds, ensueing rage, blood draws and any witnesses of such an event with an untrained eye may likely assume pure insanity at play. "Insanity is doing the same thing over and over again and expecting different results." When you gloriously stick the trick, you won't try it ever again, and hope your homie filmed it well and instead of Two to Make it True, it'll be One and Done. Not to worry, your progression will likely never come this point, just depends on how badly you want it. Most adults just want to get proficient, not compete or go pro.

Anecdotally, some of my youth students like to substitute Two to Make it True with Two to make it Poo and even took it as far as coining, Three to Make it Pee. Haha, kids..

NO PAIN, NO GAIN

If I told you that you'd never fall or get hurt skateboarding, I'd be lying to you. Skateboarding is a physical sport where we get hurt physically and sometimes emotionally. By vastly exceeding margins, my program severely limits the amount of falling to infrequent, small, calculated and oh-so-necessary baby slams. I've seen a couple of my adult students go down hard, but they are seasoned skaters trying intermediate-level tricks, thus far resulting in one ER visit (X-rays were negative) and zero broken bones (knock on wood)! I can teach you 85-90% of what you need to learn and my trusted assistance, Mr. Concrete will teach you the rest. All joking side, falling is learning and it is by far the fastest route to learning, however the curriculum is not designed to be a fast-track program, nor should it be for new adults. When you fall your brain becomes programmed to NOT make the same mistake twice. Kind of like if you ever received spankings as a kid, you know what I'm talking about. Falling is the price of learning and what a coach can't teach you or when learning goes beyond the ability to be taught properly without falling. If you decide not to try again after falling due to fear, you're wasting a learning opportunity. The best time to try again is just after a fall. The sacrifice of slamming is the lesson learned and trying again in the face of fear is so crucial when learning new tricks. I've coached a 30-something-year-old female later skater battle it out with a tough trick, over and over again she would fall and try again. With each try she was getting closer to landing it, her emotions raising, tears streaming and body trembling. It was an epic battle against fear and adversity that she won and at that moment exclaimed, "Best feeling ever!" If you can get through that, sky's the limit.

Everyone has their own pain thresholds. The higher your pain threshold the better, but there is a limit to that. Some have such high thresholds or no thresholds that they experience pleasure with pain. That can lead to unnecessary injuries and can be hard to cap. If your pain threshold is low, it's not set in stone, there are ways to increase it. The ideal pain threshold for your skateboarding, on a scale of 1 to 10, is a 7 to 8. Keep in mind the required protective gear for lessons will help tremendously. Some students also like to wear padded shorts to help with hip and tailbone falls. Other feel the need to also use a mouth guard. Protective gear will not only minimize injury, it will also build enough confidence to place two feet on your skateboard and keep going. Skateboarding is particularly hard on your ankles. There are some great yoga exercises to help with before and after skate sessions. Yoga for skaters is fantastic and you can find online classes led by yoga instructors who are also skateboarders. They focus on high-impact areas of the body including hip flexors, quads, knees, and ankles.

ABOUT THE AUTHOR

Marko Kosta, born 1975, raised in New York City, street skating in Queens and Manhattan from age 14. He attended college at Pace University, the downtown NYC campus which was situated just down the street from the Brooklyn Banks, at the time, "The Banks" was one of the most famous street skate spots in the Country. He recalls how difficult it was to focus in class when all his skate buddies were skating in the vicinity and, on the other hand, how nice it was to walk out of class and almost instantly be reconnected with friends skating some of the best street spots in the City. No need for phones or social media.

Marko spent 20 years living in the San Francisco Bay Area, where he raised his kids, worked professionally in advertising and kept skating. It was skating that originally caught his eye for the Bay Area and a career job in SF solidified his relocation from NY. He blends his Bachelor's in Business Administration with over ten years of co-leading non-profit youth development organizations, volunteering in several capacities including Skateboard Coach. This, combined with over thirty years of actual skateboarding experience and some encouragement from fellow volunteers, in 2018, Marko launched a skate school named SK8 GYM in San Francisco, California. SK8 GYM is at the intersection of Marko's three biggest passion points: teaching/ coaching, skateboarding and business administration. He has held over 10,000 hours of skate lessons/ classes, has taught over 2,500 students, with more than two-hundred of them being first-time adult skaters, aka L8R SK8RS.

SK8 GYM keeps expanding every year and throughout all this expansion, Marko's work continues to focus on skateboarding curriculum and specifically working with adults who are trying it for the very first time. If you want to see what people are saying about Marko's lessons, check out his online reviews on the SK8 GYM website. Marko travels all across the country to teach adults who are ready to take the leap.

Check us out at www.sk8gym.com for more information and to book your first skateboard lesson with Coach Marko. If you don't see your area listed, it doesn't necessarily mean we don't offer it there, just email us at info@sk8gym.com and we'll get you set up.

www.ingramcontent.com/pod-product-compliance
Lightning Source LLC
Chambersburg PA
CBHW041320110526
44591CB00021B/2855